Our CRAZY Class Election

Panel 1: "I THOUGHT YOU KNEW RUNNING FOR HOMEROOM PRESIDENT WOULD TAKE LOTS OF ENERGY." "I DID."

Panel 2: "I JUST DIDN'T KNOW RUNNING AGAINST TANK WOULD INVOLVE SO MUCH RUNNING."

GUY MALONEY

Thanks, Matt Ringler, for your help
in putting the pieces together!
—T.R.

ISBN-13: 978-0-545-00401-5
ISBN-10: 0-545-00401-2

12 11 10 9 8 7 6 5 4 3   8 9 10 11 12/0

Printed in the U.S.A.
First printing, October 2007

COMIC GUY ™

Our CRAZY Class Election

BY TIMOTHY ROLAND

Scholastic Inc.
New York   Toronto   London   Auckland   Sydney
Mexico City   New Delhi   Hong Kong   Buenos Aires

CHAPTER ONE

THE BEGINNING OF THE END

Most people would have called it a zoo. But at Rockyville Elementary School, we called it a homeroom.

Homeroom 207.

Twenty-four
fifth-grade kids.

A half-crazy teacher.

A pet iguana,
two hamsters,
and a monkey.

Mix them all together and you get lots of ideas for a comic strip.
Sometimes.
Sometimes you get a situation that isn't very funny. Like on Monday.

I was at my desk drawing a picture of my teacher, when I felt a tap on my shoulder.

"I can't believe it, Guy," said my best friend, Molly.

"That Miss Lizzy looks this funny?" I chuckled as I held up my drawing.

"No," said Molly. "I can't believe the big ape is here on time." She pointed at the muscular beast stomping into the room.

His name was Tank, and as he rumbled past my desk, his elbow banged into my head. "Watch where you're going, Comic Boy!" he growled.

"But I didn't move," I said.

He gave me a shove, then shook his fist at me as he continued down the aisle. "Just wait until I'm your president!" he sneered.

"My what?"

"I think he means he wants to run for homeroom president," explained Molly. "Remember Miss Lizzy told us about the election last Friday?"

"Oh…yeah…right." I nodded, although I had no idea what Molly was talking about. All I remembered about Friday's class was coming up with some good comic strip ideas.

I write and illustrate a comic strip called **COMIC GUY** for the school newspaper. It's about me and about what happens at school.

A good time to work on ideas for
COMIC GUY is during a boring class.
Except when I'm interrupted by Ollie.

HEY! BRING BACK
MY PICTURE!

And except when I'm interrupted by
you-know-who.

GUY MALONEY!
ARE YOU LISTENING?!

"Yes, Miss Lizzy," I answered.

"Good. Because before I begin today's
lesson, I'd like to clear up what's happening
with this Friday's election. Apparently, some of
you weren't paying attention when I explained
things last week." She looked directly at me.

I slumped in my chair.

"You will be electing a homeroom president," explained Miss Lizzy. "Tomorrow you will nominate candidates. And on Friday, you will be voting for—"

"Me!" shouted Tank. He raised his gorilla-like arms in the air, as if he had already won.

It was hard to tell who was the real monkey.

Several students groaned.

Miss Lizzy cleared her throat. Then, almost as if pleading, she said, "This is an important election. So I hope you will nominate some good candidates."

"Yeah, like that's going to happen," I whispered to Molly. "Who'd be crazy enough to run against Tank?"

Molly looked at me.

"Don't even think about it," I said. "I know what Tank is going to do to whoever runs against him."

"Unfortunately," moaned Molly, "so does everyone else."

I leaned back in my seat and listened as Miss Lizzy started her science lesson. My mind began to wander, thinking about Tank becoming president, and about what our homeroom would look like if that happened.

When class was over, Tank stood by the door and smiled. "He looks so normal," said Molly, "like he's turned over a new leaf. And like he may actually be a good homeroom president."

I glanced at Tank's smile. It did seem sincere. Maybe Molly was right. And maybe my mom was right when she said I should always give a person a chance to change. "They might surprise you," she said.

Okay. I did like surprises.

I followed Molly to the doorway. "Vote for me," said Tank. He shook Molly's hand and smiled as she stepped into the hallway.

"Vote for me," he said. He shook my hand and smiled. Then, with an apelike push, he shoved me into the hallway.

SURPRISE! (Although, not really.)

I looked up at Molly...and at the stars circling my head. "We've got to find someone to run against him," I said, "or he'll turn our zoo—I mean our homeroom—into a jungle."

"You're right," said Molly, helping me to my feet. "But who?"

CHAPTER TWO
AND THE ANSWER IS . . .

I needed some answers. Fast!

I needed to find someone to run against Tank for homeroom president. And then, there was math.

MY BIGGEST MATH PROBLEM

When I can't do the math problem, I get nervous.

When I get nervous, I can't do the math problem.

"And that's why you didn't do your math homework?" asked Molly.

"I did half the problems," I said.

"Really?" Molly gave me a look like she didn't believe me.

"Well, maybe not quite half," I admitted.

"How many did you do?" asked Molly.

"A quarter of them."

"Which is how many?"

"Three," I guessed.

"Three isn't a quarter of twenty," chuckled Molly, "five is." Then her face slowly turned serious. "Mr. Crane isn't going to be very happy with you."

"He's never happy with me," I said.

"That's because you joke around in class too much."

"It's what I do when I'm nervous," I explained. "It relieves the tension. It calms me down."

"And sometimes," said Molly, leading the way into math class, "it gets you into trouble."

13

I stepped carefully into Principal Hawk's office. I'd been there before (a few dozen times, at least), so I knew what to expect. A scolding. Detention. A warning that he didn't want to see me in his office ever again (even though we both knew he would).

Fortunately for me, you don't always get what you expect.

15

"So you're not afraid of Tank?" I asked.

Clint stuck out his chin and grinned like a tiger. "I'm not afraid of anyone...or anything!"

"Just wait until you face the cafeteria's food," I chuckled.

"What?"

"You'll see," I said. "But right now we're about to face something even more terrifying." As I walked next to Clint, I explained about the election for homeroom president, and about Tank wanting to run.

"Then someone needs to run against him," said Clint. "Someone brave. Someone with lots of ideas. Someone who would be a good leader."

"And who do you suggest?" I asked.

Clint grinned at me like a candidate ready to leap into action.

I smiled back, because it was the answer I was looking for. And finding it was easy. At least, easier than finding the answers to my still-unfinished math homework.

CHAPTER THREE
I WAITED FOR THIS?

On Tuesday morning, I couldn't wait to hop out of bed. I couldn't wait to finish breakfast. I couldn't wait to get to school. "Hey, Guy!" yelled Molly. "Couldn't you wait for me?!"

I turned and saw my best friend stampeding toward me like an angry rhino. "Oops...sorry," I said.

Molly and I are neighbors.

And we always walk to school together.

Or run to school together.

Or in the winter, slide to school together.

"So what's the big rush, Guy?" asked Molly as we approached our school.

"I can't wait to see Tank's face when he finds out someone will be running against him."

"You mean Clint?"

I nodded.

"He told you he wanted to run?"

"Sort of."

"Well," said Molly while stepping into our homeroom, "it was nice knowing him."

"What do you mean by that?" I asked. Of course, I knew exactly what she meant.

I sat down at my desk, which was right in front of Clint's. "Ready?" I asked him.

"Ready," he replied.

Then we listened as Miss Lizzy explained.

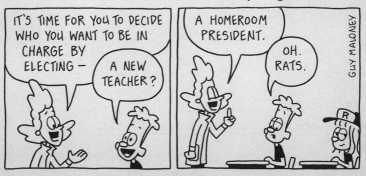

TODAY YOU WILL BE NOMINATING CANDIDATES TO RUN FOR THE OFFICE OF HOMEROOM PRESIDENT.

TO NOMINATE SOMEONE, RAISE YOUR HAND AND TELL ME WHO YOU WANT TO BE A CANDIDATE.

BUT YOU SAID WE COULD NOMINATE ANYONE TO RUN FOR HOMEROOM PRESIDENT.

I KNOW, MR. ZAPPERONI, BUT WHAT I MEANT WAS...

...ANYONE HUMAN.

SORRY, OLLIE, BUT I TRIED.

YES, TANK, THE HOMEROOM PRESIDENT MUST BE SOMEONE WHO LIKES TO BE IN CHARGE AND TAKE CONTROL OF THINGS.

SO WHO WOULD YOU LIKE TO NOMINATE FOR THE POSITION?

ME.

GUY MAIONEY

GUY MAIONEY

20

There was silence as everyone waited.

Of course, it was all part of my plan. To let the tension build. To let everyone think that Tank was the only one running for homeroom president.

Then, I'd raise my hand and nominate Clint. And I'd listen to the sighs of relief. And I'd watch Tank's face scrunch up like that of an angry gorilla who didn't know what hit him.

"You think it's time?" asked Clint, poking me in the back.

"Almost," I answered.

"Well, we need a candidate to run against Tank."

"I know."

"Someone tough."

"Yeah."

"Who isn't afraid to stand up to Tank."

I looked back at Clint and smiled. "Okay," I said, "let's do it."

But before I could raise my hand, Clint's hand shot into the air. "Miss Lizzy," he said in a strong, clear voice. "I would like to nominate Guy Maloney for the office of homeroom president."

WHO?   ME?

CHAPTER FOUR

WE'RE ALL BEHIND YOU

It happened so fast. And when it was over, all I could say was,

"Then why didn't you tell Miss Lizzy you didn't want to run?" asked Molly.

"I don't know."

"Did your brain freeze?"

I scratched my head, then nodded. .

"And now look at the mess I'm in," I said,

walking with Molly to our lockers. "You think I can convince Miss Lizzy my nomination was all a big mistake?"

"Nope. Too late. You have to run," said Molly.

"Why?" I looked at Molly. Then I spotted Clint rolling closer. "Hey, what happened in there?" I growled.

"What do you mean?" asked Clint.

"I thought you wanted to run," I said.

"I did."

"Then why didn't you wait for me to nominate you?"

Clint shrugged. "It doesn't matter now. What matters is that someone's running against Tank."

"But I don't want to run!" I screamed. "And besides, I don't even know how."

"That's why I'm here," said Clint. "I'm going to manage your campaign. And together we'll show our classmates that what they need is a good leader."

"Like Guy Maloney?" chuckled Molly. She looked at me, then fell down laughing.

I chuckled, too. It was a good joke—one I could use in **COMIC GUY**.

MOUNT RUSHMORE (PLUS ONE MORE).

"But this isn't a laughing matter," scolded Clint. "Elections are supposed to be serious."

"And fun," said Molly. "Although this one would be more fun if Guy wasn't running against—" Her mouth dropped open. Her eyes widened. She pointed behind me.

I turned and saw a growling Tank. But before he could do anything, Zoe stepped out from behind his hulking body. "This is for the school newspaper," she said, holding up her camera. "So let's do it in one shot." She pushed Tank and me together. "Now shake!" she ordered.

Tank grabbed my hand and smiled. I smiled, too. I knew the big ape wasn't stupid enough to try something with a camera focused on him.

But I was wrong.

Zoe led Tank away for a newspaper interview. "I'll schedule one for you later, Guy," she yelled back to me.

I nodded. Then, when she was out of sight, I let out a scream as I looked down at my throbbing hand. It felt like it had been squashed in a huge vise.

"And that," said Molly, "is why you must run, and why you must win—so Tank doesn't become our homeroom president!"

I looked at my best friend. Unfortunately, she was right.

CHAPTER FIVE
SPEECHLESS NO MORE

There were three big problems with me being a candidate for homeroom president.

1. I DIDN'T WANT TO RUN!

2. Tank was running against me.
   (Which meant he would soon
     be running over me.)

3. I had to give a speech.

"Just thinking about it makes me sweat," I explained to Clint. "And it makes the words inside my head get jumbled up like they always do when I stand in front of a crowd full of kids staring directly at me."

"And that's why you don't want to give a speech?" asked Clint.

"Yeah. That, plus I have no idea what to say."

We prepared for the speech while sitting at a table in the cafeteria. I had nothing to eat, since Ollie (again!) had swiped my bag lunch. So Clint gave me half his grilled cheese sandwich—along with his thoughts on the upcoming speech.

"You can do it if you believe you can," said Clint.

"That's easy for you to say." I took a big bite of my sandwich. Cheese oozed out onto my chin.

"Close your eyes," ordered Clint, "and pretend you're about to give your speech. Now picture in your mind a leader, someone who would make a great homeroom president." He paused for a moment. "Okay, who do you see?"

YOU.

NO. YOU'RE SUPPOSED TO SEE YOU!

"But you would make the best homeroom president," I said. "You're good at taking control. You know what you're doing. So why aren't you the candidate?"

"Because I'm not," answered Clint.

"Why?" I looked at Clint. Then, without thinking, I asked, "Are you afraid to run?"

Clint glared at me like an angry tiger. "I'm not afraid of anything!" he roared. Then he threw the speech in my lap and wheeled himself away.

Yeah, it was a stupid thing for me to ask. I already knew Clint was tough and fearless. But what I didn't know was that by homeroom period at the end of the day, he would roll beside me like the incident never happened.

"I don't get it," I said. "What's going on?"

"You're about to give a speech," answered Clint.

"I mean, with you?"

"I'm getting you ready for your speech," said Clint, trying to change the subject. "Did you read it?"

"Yes," I answered.

"Any questions?"

I scratched my head. Everything was happening so fast. "Well," I said, "I'm still not exactly sure what a homeroom president does."

"He gives speeches," said Clint, pushing me toward the front of the room.

CHAPTER SIX

DID I SAY THAT?

It happened right after Miss Lizzy announced I would be speaking first. I stepped nervously to the front of the room. I looked at Miss Lizzy, at my classmates, at my speech. Then I opened my mouth.

Nothing.

I tried again. Same result. No voice. Which meant no speech. It was terrible news.

Although not everyone agreed.

"And he wants to be our homeroom president?" laughed Tank. "Look at him. He's supposed to be giving a speech, and he's joking around...again."

"No, he's not," argued Clint. Then he turned toward me and asked, "Are you?"

I shook my head back and forth.

"Well, if he can't give his speech," said Tank,

"he can't run. Which means, I automatically win the election!"

There were several gasps in the room.

Clint rolled closer to Tank. "But he *can* give his speech."

"Without a voice?" snarled Tank.

"I'll be his voice," said Clint.

"What?" asked Tank.

"What?" I tried (unsuccessfully) to ask.

"What?" asked Miss Lizzy.

Clint quickly explained his plan to our teacher. He would sit behind me as I stood in front of the class. "And," he said, "I'll read the speech that I—I mean, that Guy—wrote."

Miss Lizzy smiled. She loved experiments and told us we could try it.

Clint rolled behind me. "Open and close your mouth as I read," he whispered. "It will give everyone the impression that you're the one giving the speech." After the first few sentences, it seemed to be working.

35

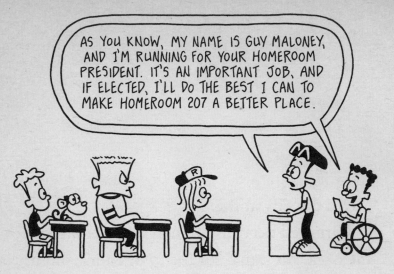

The speech continued with me (I mean Clint) explaining what I would do.

1. Organize the class so we all worked together.
2. Identify problems and try to bring about change.
3. Represent Homeroom 207.

36

"Ha!" Tank jumped up from his seat. "How can you be our voice, when you don't have one of your own?"

"Please don't interrupt," said Clint (as I continued to move my mouth).

"You gonna stop me?" roared Tank. He glared directly at me.

I grinned nervously. Then Clint poked me in the back, his signal for me to open my mouth.

"That's telling him, Guy!" yelled Molly. Several kids clapped.

Tank steamed toward me. "Nobody talks to me like that! Especially a squirt like you, Guy Maloney!" He shoved his face into mine and growled, as if waiting for me to apologize.

Unfortunately, I couldn't.

Fortunately, Miss Lizzy stepped in to break things up. She sent Tank back to his seat. Then she turned toward me. "Guy Maloney, you know better than to call people names!" She crossed her arms and scowled. "What do you have to say for yourself?"

I wanted to remind Miss Lizzy it wasn't me who had talked, but I

For once in my life, I was in trouble for not talking!

couldn't. Then I felt a poke in my back.

"I say," said Clint (as I opened my mouth), "that if elected, I'll work to bring about freedom from the fear of being bullied by...well, you know who. So vote for me, Guy Maloney, for homeroom president."

Miss Lizzy smiled.

The classroom exploded—in applause. And as I walked to my seat, everyone congratulated me on the speech (which I didn't give).

I watched and listened as Tank stomped to the front of the room and growled out his speech. "I'm Tank. I'm running for homeroom president. Vote for me—or else!" His hands tightened into fists. Then he shot me a fiery glare that said, "Get ready, punk, for the toughest campaign in the history of Rockyville Elementary School elections!"

CHAPTER SEVEN
THE QUEEN AND ME

When homeroom period was over, Zoe ordered me to follow her to the beehive.

The beehive is what I call the newspaper room.

—Because it is always swarming with activity.

—Because everyone works together (like bees) for a common goal (publishing the school newspaper).

—Because Zoe (the newspaper's editor) orders her workers around like a queen bee.

"Sit down!" ordered Zoe.

I sat on a chair and looked around. Kids were busy preparing articles for the next issue of the school newspaper.

I pulled a new **COMIC GUY** comic strip from my backpack. "Here," I said, handing it to Zoe. "You don't want to forget to include the most popular feature."

Zoe snarled. But she knew I was right. Which is why she allowed **COMIC GUY** in the paper.

Everyone loved **COMIC GUY** — except for Zoe. She said I needed to make it more serious. So I added her to my strip.

ZOE'S VERSION OF WHY SHE DOESN'T LIKE COMIC STRIPS.

BECAUSE I HAVE A BRAIN.

MY VERSION OF WHY ZOE DOESN'T LIKE COMIC STRIPS.

BECAUSE YOU'RE MISSING A BONE.

A FUNNY BONE.

GUY MALONEY

"All right, time for your interview," said
Zoe. She pulled out a reporter's notebook and
a pencil. "So tell me, Guy, why do you want to
become homeroom president?"

"I don't," I answered.

"You don't?"

"No," I said, watching Zoe scratch her head.
Then I explained.

"What?!" Zoe narrowed her eyes and pointed
her nose directly at me. "Is this one of your
jokes, Maloney?"

"No," I answered.

"Then explain why, if you don't want to run,
anyone should vote for you."

"So Tank doesn't become homeroom president," I replied.

"Actually," said Zoe, "that's a good reason."

As Zoe jotted down some notes, I decided to test her famous brain. "So who's going to win the election?" I asked.

"No one knows," she replied.

"But I thought you knew everything," I chuckled.

Zoe sneered. "You can't count votes until they're cast," she explained. "But you can take a poll, which is what I did for the newspaper."

"A poll?" I asked.

"Yes," said Zoe. "I asked ten kids how they planned to vote." She showed me a piece of paper. "And here are the results."

→ 5 are voting for Guy.

→ 2 are voting for Tank.

→ 3 are undecided.

"Which means you should get how much of the vote?" asked Zoe.

"A quarter?" I guessed.

"No. One-half!" Zoe rolled her eyes. "Five is one-half of ten. Don't you know anything?"

My cheeks grew warm as I tried to grin. "Actually," I said, "math isn't one of my strong points."

"No fooling," said Zoe. "And neither is running for homeroom president."

"If you ask me," said Zoe, "a monkey would make just as good a homeroom president as either you or Tank."

"I agree," said Zapper as he stepped into the newspaper room. He stood in front of us and unzipped his backpack. Ollie jumped out, ran over, and shook my hand.

DON'T MONKEY AROUND! VOTE FOR THE MONKEY!

"For what?" I asked.

"Homeroom president," answered Zapper.

I scratched my head. "But Miss Lizzy said—"

"That Ollie couldn't be nominated," interrupted Zapper. "But that doesn't mean he can't run as a write-in candidate."

"What's that?" I asked.

"When the kids vote," explained Zapper, "they can write Ollie's name on the ballot instead of yours or Tank's."

"They can do that?" I asked.

"Why not?" said Zapper.

We both looked at Zoe for an answer. But all she did was smile. "This is going to be a crazy election," she said, picking up her reporter's notebook, "which should make for some interesting news."

THE BARKER

Rockyville Elementary School News

NEW CANDIDATE SWINGS INTO ACTION

   The race for Homeroom 207 president has tightened. According to a new poll, if the election were held today, 40% of the class would vote for Guy, 30% for Ollie, 20% for Tank, and 10% are undecided.

   "But those numbers will change by Friday," warned Tank. "Because no one is going to make a monkey out of me!"

CHAPTER EIGHT

LET THE EXPLOSION BEGIN

The math was easy—even for me.

"If Ollie picks up just a few more votes by Friday," explained Clint, "he'll become homeroom president."

"And I'll be off the hook," I said, grinning.

"No, you won't," said Clint.

"Why not?"

"Because we're going to stop him from running. Come on!" He gave my arm a tug, then zoomed down the hallway toward our homeroom. On the way we met up with Tank, who for once was thinking the exact same thing as Clint.

STOP THAT MONKEY!!

We rushed into our homeroom.

"Hold it right there!" ordered Miss Lizzy. "I'm in the middle of an experiment!"

Miss Lizzy was always experimenting, which was why she was known around school as "the crazy scientist." But she was also a teacher. From her we learned:

1. To be prepared for anything.

2. How to evacuate the room quickly.

3. How to clean up the mess before Principal Hawk found out what happened.

"Okay, come over," said Miss Lizzy. "But slowly."

Tank, Clint, and I moved cautiously toward the lab table. Miss Lizzy held a tube containing red liquid in one hand. With her other hand, she pointed to a jar of blue liquid on the table. "Do you know what's going to happen when I mix these two ingredients together?" she asked.

"No," we all answered.

"Neither do I." She grinned, then poured the ingredients together.

I stepped back and got ready to run. I had a pretty good idea of what was about to happen.

The mixture turned purple. And bubbled.

And began to smoke.

And... then, it stopped.

UH, OH.

I'M OUT OF HERE!

HUH?

"Hmm. Interesting," said Miss Lizzy. She jotted down a few notes, then looked at us. "So what did you want to see me about?"

"Ollie's a monkey!" shouted Tank.

"I know," said Miss Lizzy.

"And you're letting him run?" asked Clint.

"Yes. I changed my mind." Miss Lizzy grinned like she did before one of her experiments. "I'm letting the voters decide if they want him for homeroom president. I'm letting them have another choice. And I'm sure they'll choose wisely."

"Our classmates?" said Clint.

"Are you kidding?!" shouted Tank.

"All I'm doing is mixing things up a bit," explained Miss Lizzy. "And just like in my experiments, everything will turn out all right." Her grin widened as she poured something green into the jar of purple liquid on the lab table.

I watched the mixture turn brown. Then bubble. Then smoke. Then—

CHAPTER NINE

READY! SET! CAMPAIGN!

My plan was simple.

1. I would keep moving so Tank would never catch me (or at least never catch me alone).

2. I would try to get out of being a candidate.

3. If I couldn't, I'd let Clint handle all the details of my campaign.

Clint was the brains of my campaign.
He directed the action. He answered my
questions. Except the one I kept asking:
"Why aren't *you* running?"

Molly was in charge of publicity. And charge
was what she did, racing full-speed ahead to

make sure my campaign
posters ended up everywhere
(which they did).

But for me, campaigning wasn't easy. It was
like being in a three-ring circus, with me, Tank,
and Ollie all in different rings at the same time
trying to attract the attention of voters.

There was action, confusion, and humor.
Here are some of the highlights (and lowlights)
of the campaign.

CHAPTER TEN

GIVE THEM WHAT THEY WANT

By Thursday, all three campaigns were barreling ahead at full speed.

— Tank was using strong-arm tactics to try to bully his way to victory.

— Ollie was targeting the swing vote (meaning, those who might vote for a swinger).

— I was being guided (or rather, pushed) by Clint and Molly to maintain my lead.

"We've got to get serious if we want to win," said Clint. "So no more fooling around." He looked at me. Then he glared at Molly. "And no more vote-for-Guy blizzards."

"But it almost worked," she said.

Clint rolled his eyes. Then both he and Molly gave me advice on what to do to win.

I smiled at each of them (even though I wanted to tell them that for me, getting out of the campaign was the best policy). Then I watched as Clint left to work on my last speech.

"Okay. Now let's do it!" said Molly, grabbing my arm.

"What?" I asked.

"Get more votes."

"But according to Zoe's latest newspaper

poll, I'm already winning," I reminded her. "And like Clint said, we don't want to do anything to mess that up."

"But you can do better! You can get *all* the votes!" Molly squinted her eyes, focused straight ahead, and tilted her hat so she looked like a charging rhino who no one could stop. Including me.

"All you have to do is make promises," she  explained. "Find out what a voter wants or needs, and then promise you'll make it happen."

"But what if I know I can't keep the promise?" I asked.

"Doesn't matter," chuckled Molly. "Because the voter won't know that...until *after* the election."

"But isn't that dishon—"

"Look!" interrupted Molly. "There's Tiffany." She tugged my arm. "Come on, Guy, let's go make her a promise!"

"You voting for Guy in the election?" asked Molly, stepping in front of Tiffany.

"I don't know," she answered. She brushed her hair so it fell in a perfectly straight line behind her back. "Right now, I have more important things to think about."

"Like what?" asked Molly.

"Like getting ready for our class picture," answered Tiffany.

"But that's not for another week and a half," said Molly.

THE (ALMOST) NEW TIFFANY

— new shirt
— new purse
— new skirt
— new shoes
— same old half-empty head

"I know," complained Tiffany. "Not much time to get ready, is there?" She opened the fashion magazine she was holding. "You think I should wear a pink dress or a red one? Or maybe a blue one? Or maybe new shoes? Or—"

"What you need," said Molly, putting her hand over Tiffany's mouth, "is more time. Like maybe having off from school the day before the class picture so you can get ready."

Tiffany's eyes brightened. "You could make that happen?"

"No. But Guy could. And he will." Molly pointed at me. "If you vote for him and he becomes homeroom president."

"Then I will," gushed Tiffany. She smiled at me, and for a moment looked like she was about to kiss me. (Yuck!) Fortunately, all she did was shake my hand and skip away.

IT'S A DEAL!

"See how easy that was?" asked Molly.

"Yes," I said, "but—"

"It's the way all the politicians do it, Guy," explained Molly. "At least all the ones who want to win elections. And you do want to win, don't you?" She stared at me and nodded.

"Yes," I said, nodding my head, too. "I do."

"Good." She gave me a shove. "Then it's time for you to get out there and make some promises."

CHAPTER ELEVEN

AND THAT'S A PROMISE!

It didn't seem right. But I kept telling myself
I would do it....

During lunch, I slid onto a cafeteria bench
next to several classmates. At first I had a hard
time knowing what to promise. But then it got
easier...and easier. And as I made more
promises, I began to promise more...and
more...and—

68

Like Molly said, making campaign promises was easy. And by the time I finished, I was doing it...

"So how was it?" asked Molly as she joined me for an after lunch walk back to class.

"Terrible. I think I'm gonna be sick," I said. "The meatloaf was mushy, the mashed potatoes lumpy, the vegetables cold, and—"

"Not the lunch!" scolded Molly. "I mean, how did making promises go?"

"Good," I said.

"And you got more votes?" asked Molly.

"I think so," I said. Then I grinned.

It was like I was
Santa Claus
giving away gifts.

Or like a king
who could grant
any request.

"Or like a Guy," said Molly, "who now wants to become homeroom president."

As I looked at her, a strange feeling rumbled through my stomach. Maybe because I was digesting what she said. Or maybe because I was having trouble digesting my lunch.

"It's called having power," explained Molly. She smiled and nudged me with her elbow. "Feels good, doesn't it?"

"Yes," I admitted. "It does."

"And after tomorrow," she said, putting her hand on my shoulder, "you'll have power all the time. Because nothing can stop you from being elected homeroom president. Not Tank. Not Ollie."

"Then how about me?" said an angry voice behind me.

I spun around and got smacked by a purse.

"OUCH!"

"How could you promise Louis you'd cancel the class picture," blasted Tiffany, "when you promised me extra time to get ready for it?!" She smacked me again with her purse.

"OUCH!"

Steam rose from her head, just like it did from one of Miss Lizzy's experiments right before . . . well, you know what.

Molly shot me a scolding stare. "You didn't keep track of your promises?"

"I got carried away," I said.

"Hmph!" huffed Tiffany. She straightened her hair, then stuck her face closer to mine. "Guy Maloney, you're nothing but a dirty rotten double-crosser!"

I grinned nervously and braced for another purse smack. "OUCH!"

"Actually," explained Molly, stepping between me and Tiffany, "Guy's just a candidate who doesn't know how to make promises."

"You mean, doesn't know how to *keep* promises!" hissed Tiffany. She turned to walk away, then glanced back. "But I do. And today I'm going to tell everyone what you've done. And tomorrow, you definitely won't be getting my vote. AND THAT'S A PROMISE!"

THE BARKER

Rockyville Elementary School News

CANDIDATE STUMBLES

The race for Homeroom 207 president is now too close to call. By making too many unrealistic promises, Guy angered several voters and threw away his comfortable lead. A new poll taken after the candidate's blunder shows that Guy lost votes, Tank gained votes, and Ollie was still the monkey in the middle.

YOU LOST YOUR LEAD BECAUSE YOU MADE TOO MANY PROMISES.

SO DON'T MAKE ANY MORE!

I WON'T. I PROMISE.

GUY MALONEY

CHAPTER TWELVE
SHOWDOWN

It was Friday—election day. Finally!

I stood by my locker waiting for Clint to bring my final speech. He was late, which gave me time to sort through my thoughts.

Some days my head is filled with useful thoughts. Some days it's not. Friday was a "not" day.

But I needed an idea (and QUICKLY!), because I was headed toward trouble. Or rather, trouble was headed toward me...

...like a bull toward a bull's-eye.

"Well, well, well," said Tank, slamming his right fist against my locker and smiling. "If it isn't the **COMIC GUY**. Alone...at last." He slammed his left fist on the other side of me so I couldn't escape.

I looked around, then at Tank. Sweat dripped down my neck. "What do you want, Tank?" I asked in a shaky voice.

"To win the election!" he replied. "To become president! To take over our homeroom!"

"And then what?" I asked.

Tank paused, scratched his empty apelike head, then glared at me again. "Don't try to confuse me!" he growled. "'Cause what I want right now is for you to drop out of the election!" He aimed his right fist at my face. "Or else!"

I didn't have to ask, "Or else what?" I knew. Which is why I shut my eyes and waited for the KA-POW! But all I heard was a KA-BUMP!

"Leave him alone!" shouted Clint. KA-BUMP! He rammed Tank again. Then Tank whirled around and the two glared...

…and glared…and glared…and glared, until finally Tank blinked and stomped away.

I wiped some sweat from my brow and looked over at Clint. "What just happened?" I asked.

"What matters," said Clint, "is what's about to happen. Because you're about to give your final campaign speech."

My knees shook for a moment as I thought about it. Then I looked down the hallway and watched Tank disappear into our homeroom. "Is he afraid of you?" I asked Clint, still trying to believe what I saw.

EVERYONE'S AFRAID OF SOMETHING.

REALLY? SO WHAT ARE YOU AFRAID OF?

Clint didn't answer. He handed me my speech, which I quickly looked at. "Have any questions?" he asked.

I did. But not about the speech.

"But kids won't vote for me because I'm different," explained Clint, pointing to his wheelchair.

"We're all different," I said. "But all anyone cares about in the election is who will do the best job. And that's you!" I moved in front of the wheelchair and stared at him.

"Are you afraid of running for homeroom president?"

"Are you afraid of giving a speech?" he asked, staring back.

"Yes, I am," I admitted. "But I'm still going to try. And so should you."

CHAPTER THIRTEEN

THE FINAL PITCH

We were late for homeroom period (but unfortunately, not for my speech). We were also (according to Clint) too late to switch candidates. "If we change, we risk messing things up and allowing Tank to win," he warned. "So let's not rock the boat."

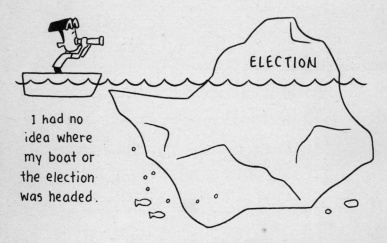

ELECTION

I had no idea where my boat or the election was headed.

"All right, class, quiet down!" ordered Miss Lizzy. "It's time for the experiment—I mean, the election." Her smile widened. "But first, we'll hear from the candidates one last time."

She called on Ollie, who was carried to
the front of the room in a box by Zapper.
He set the box on the floor. "And now," he
announced, "it's time to go bananas!" He
opened the
box and out
jumped Ollie.

"'Honest
Ollie' is the
candidate who
makes promises
he'll keep," said
He was dressed to look like
President Abraham Lincoln.

Zapper. He glanced at me, then back at the
class. "And if elected, Ollie promises you'll get
a banana on every lunch tray." Ollie threw
bananas to the class as Zapper held up a chart.

"And instead of letter grades," continued
Zapper, "you'll get bananas."

THE BANANA GRADING SYSTEM

A = ⫰⫰⫰⫰ 4 bananas

B = ⫰⫰⫰ 3 bananas

C = ⫰⫰ 2 bananas

D = ⫰ 1 banana

F = ⌒ 1 banana peel

"So vote for 'Honest Ollie' to be your homeroom president!" said Zapper.

I listened to the applause as I ate a banana. It was a goofy campaign strategy. But sometimes goofy works.

Tank's speech was next. Although I had to

look twice to figure out who walked to the front
of the room.

THE NEW IMPROVED TANK

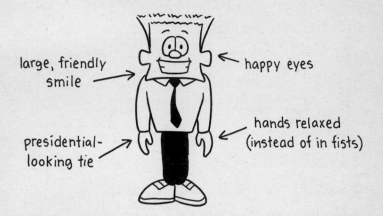

large, friendly
smile

happy eyes

presidential-
looking tie

hands relaxed
(instead of in fists)

"What's he doing?" I asked in a whisper
to Clint.

"He changed his image," replied Clint,
"to try to fool everyone into thinking he's a
nice guy."

"Think it will work?"

Clint shrugged and gave me a worried look.

"Unlike my opponents, I'm not here to make
promises I won't be able to keep," said Tank in
a pleasant-sounding voice. He glanced at me,

then at Ollie, then back at the class. "I'm here to tell you that if I'm elected president, I'll do my best to make this the number-one homeroom in the school." He paused and smiled.

Several kids smiled back.

His plan was working. And it probably would have succeeded, except that Tank couldn't keep the bully part of himself inside. It was like trying to hold back a sneeze.

THE NEW
IMPROVED TANK

THE OLD
BULLY TANK

I heard a few gasps, then silence as Tank walked to his seat. "You think he has a chance of winning?" I whispered back to Clint.

"Depends on your speech," replied Clint. "The voters need to hear from someone who doesn't make bad promises. They need to see that there's a better candidate to vote for than Tank or Ollie."

"You're right," I said as an idea popped into my head.

CHAPTER FOURTEEN
THE END OF THE BEGINNING

As I stood in front of
the classroom, I kept
telling myself not to be afraid.
But when I looked at all the
faces staring at me, my knees
shook. And my hands shook.
And when I opened my
mouth, my voice shook. But at least (this time)
it was working.

At first there was silence.
Then a few claps.
Then a warm round of applause as everyone

turned and looked at the newest candidate in the race for homeroom president.

"Clint can't be in the election!" shouted Tank.

"Why not?" asked Miss Lizzy.

"He's not a candidate!"

"He's a write-in candidate," I said, "like Ollie." Then I grinned. "I mean, like Ollie... but better."

"Exactly," said Miss Lizzy. She smiled as she walked to the front of the room. "And that's why the election is like an experiment. You need to start with the right ingredients to get the right result."

ELECTION INGREDIENTS

TANK	OLLIE	CLINT	GUY
the tough	the silly	the new	the ex-
candidate	candidate	candidate	candidate

"Vote for who you think will make the best homeroom president," said Miss Lizzy to the class. She passed out small pieces of paper. A few minutes later, she collected them and began counting votes.

HOW DARE YOU RUN AGAINST ME, YOU LITTLE CREEP! WHO DO YOU THINK YOU ARE?!

ACCORDING TO THE VOTES, WHICH HAVE NOW BEEN COUNTED, HE'S THE NEW HOMEROOM PRESIDENT.

I gave Clint a pat on the back.

Tank gave him the angry glare of a sore loser.

Ollie gave him a banana and a ham sandwich (which looked like the one missing from my lunch bag).

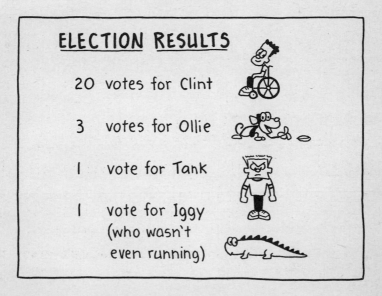

The first thing Clint did as homeroom president was offer me a job. "Are you crazy?" I replied. "I can't be vice president."

"Sure you can," said Clint.

"No, I can't," I said, "because I don't know what a vice president does."

"He takes over my job when I get sick," explained Clint.

"But I can't do that!"

"Yes, you can," said Clint, "because I never get sick. So your job as homeroom vice president will be to do nothing."

I paused, then grinned. "I can do that."

"It's what Guy does best," chuckled Molly as she stepped beside me. Everyone laughed—including me.

It was a great idea—me being homeroom vice president. Because after a long, hard-fought election, the thing I was looking forward to doing, was doing nothing. And, of course, creating more comic strips.

B I **ASK** **QUESTIONS**.

C I **THINK** about what happens.

D I **WRITE DOWN** my thoughts and ideas.

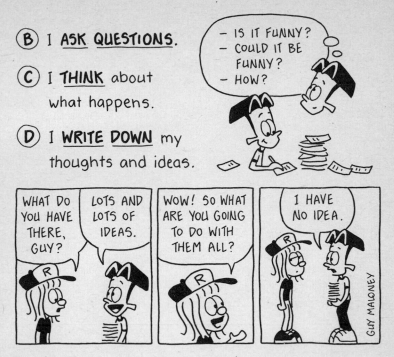

Actually, I do know what I'm going to do with my ideas. I'm going to turn them into comic strips. (Which is what I just did with my idea about collecting ideas.)

And you can create comic strips, too. But first, you need to start collecting ideas.

Learn more about creating comic strips by reading Lesson Two: "Making Your Ideas Funny," found in **COMIC GUY** Book #2.

About the Author/Illustrator

Timothy Roland never ran for homeroom
president. Probably because he was too busy
drawing funny pictures—of his teachers!
Later, when he became an elementary school
art teacher, he taught his students how to
draw funny pictures—of their teacher!

Timothy lives in Pennsylvania where he
still draws funny pictures and writes funny
stories for his new children's book series,
COMIC GUY.

COMING SOON:

COMIC GUY #2
A SILLY SCIENCE
EXPERIMENT

"What if . . . somehow . . .
all the experiments flop?"
Miss Lizzy grinned. "That's not going to
happen. Not with my students, who, like
always are going to do their very best."

"To mess things up," chuckled Tank softly.
I glanced at his shifty eyes, then back at
Miss Lizzy.